THE WAY WITH CHILDREN

ANCIENT WISDOM FOR LEADING
MODERN YOUNG PEOPLE

M. SHAYNE GALLAGHER

ILLUSTRATIONS BY
JOSH STEADMAN

BALBOA.
PRESS

A DIVISION OF HAY HOUSE

Balboa Press books may be ordered through booksellers or by contacting:

Balboa Press
A Division of Hay House
1663 Liberty Drive
Bloomington, IN 47403
www.balboapress.com
1 (877) 407-4847

Because of the dynamic nature of the Internet, any web addresses or
links contained in this book may have changed since publication and
may no longer be valid. The views expressed in this work are solely those
of the author and do not necessarily reflect the views of the publisher,
and the publisher hereby disclaims any responsibility for them.

The author of this book does not dispense medical advice or prescribe the use
of any technique as a form of treatment for physical, emotional, or medical
problems without the advice of a physician, either directly or indirectly. The
intent of the author is only to offer information of a general nature to help
you in your quest for emotional and spiritual well-being. In the event you use
any of the information in this book for yourself, which is your constitutional
right, the author and the publisher assume no responsibility for your actions.

Any people depicted in stock imagery provided by Thinkstock are
models, and such images are being used for illustrative purposes only.
Certain stock imagery © Thinkstock.

Print information available on the last page.

ISBN: 978-1-5043-7713-3 (sc)
ISBN: 978-1-5043-7715-7 (hc)
ISBN: 978-1-5043-7714-0 (e)

Library of Congress Control Number: 2017904183

Balboa Press rev. date: 08/22/2017

Contents

Foreword

Someone once said that everyone you will ever meet has the potential to become your teacher because everyone knows something that you don't. Thus, the opportunity to be a student is an ongoing one, if you are willing to open yourself up to learn what is available to you. The corollary to this is that with others you meet, you are afforded the opportunity to teach because you will always know something that they don't. What then becomes most important in those moments of contact are two questions: What do I know that can be useful and valuable for this person to learn? And what can I learn from this person in this moment that can be useful and valuable to me?

The best teachers always know that learning is teaching and vice versa and that the greatest progress is made when those of like minds seek the answers to questions together, each contributing their own knowledge, experience, and hard-won wisdom to the pursuit of their goals. As a child, I had always had mentor figures, usually teachers or family friends or older relatives to whom I looked for answers. But as a teenager, when I first became friends with Shayne Gallagher, I first realized a peer could be a teacher as well—and more, a fellow traveler both in life and in the Way.

In our early gatherings of the student group we called Excalibur, we took questions we had asked privately and shared them with one another. In asking the questions, we were able to winnow down the reasons each of us had chosen to join. Many of us were there to find ways to improve our lives, our happiness, and our self-worth. Some were there for social reasons because they thought we were some kind of elite group (or wanted to be). They quickly fell away. Some wanted the interaction, the friendship, and the sense of inclusion, which was as valid a reason as any, and maybe the best reason for a high school club to exist at all. But some of us were there because we were asking deep questions on subjects our teachers had neither the time nor the inclination to address—at least, not at the same level of sincerity with which we were asking.

We were asking questions about purpose and being, about what it meant to be alive, and perhaps most significantly, about whether it was a journey of learning we were meant to take alone or if we could walk that path with others, helping them when we could and being helped by them in turn. Shayne and I figured out very quickly that we were meant to be fellow travelers and that we would help each other whenever and wherever we could.

In those subsequent discussions, both with the Excalibur group and just as often between the two of us, we discovered Emerson and Thoreau and Dag Hammarskjold and James Allen. We learned principles of living that we strove to put into practice, and each delighted in sharing new discovery of another mentor-figure or book or essay where there was more wisdom we could incorporate into our talks. At about that time, Shayne found the Tao and Lao Tzu.

One concept we discussed has never left me. I was deeply immersed in my burgeoning comic book career and wanted to include all my friends, so Shayne and I discussed (and I even advertised in a poster and at a trade show) a comics project called SELFQUEST. It would be a comic book with a purpose: entertaining fiction, but also sharing principles of living in a way that we felt was meaningful—a method used to tremendous success by Paulo Coelho.

One of the scenes Shayne described involved a teacher suddenly appearing along the road, answering all of our protagonist's questions and displaying an amazing array of physical skills and prowess. The protagonist, astonished, asked if what he was witnessing could be taught, and the teacher responded, "You already know everything that I do. All I can do is help you find a way to remember that you know it."

Years later, I heard this same principle from one of my own mentors, Dr. Wayne Dyer, who found that all of his learning in life had led him to the Tao. He called it *satori*, or "instant awakening": a willingness to open yourself up to accepting that you know more than you realize you do; an understanding that living is learning; and an acceptance that we are already students of the Way, and teachers too. Satori helped me to understand that scene I had carried around with me since I was a teenager, and I realized that satori was possible only when you also accept that an instant awakening brings with it a responsibility to share what you know—that is, to teach.

Shayne has always been a teacher. His path in life has followed the Way better than that of almost anyone I know. I came to it later. I followed my own bliss, creating stories and art that people loved, and only realized later that the lessons I had learned along the course of my life had a value of their own, and sharing those lessons could change people's lives more than almost anything I chose to undertake.

Shayne has worked with young people from the very beginning, but now, in writing *The Way with Children*, he has found a means to share his own lessons and his own learning on a truly global scale. Now he can teach more than just the people he works with directly; now he has a greater opportunity to learn than ever before; and now, decades after we sat together in those classrooms, talking about where we would go and what we would do, I know exactly where he is: walking next to me, following the Way, just where he has always been.

May your journey be as rewarding as ours has been—and continues to be.

James A. Owen
Silvertown, Arizona

It was late in the evening. A hodgepodge group of high school kids from freshmen to seniors sat at a circle of desks in the unlocked classroom lent them for a solemn purpose of their own design. Each was there for a heartfelt and personal reason; each was there hoping to find something, or at least to seek it. No schoolteacher was in the room; they were there to teach each other. Many masters and sages were discussed over the year in these evening sessions. That evening's focus would be on the ideas of an old man from China. So the book was opened.

The Legend of Lao Tzu

Born at or around 600 BC, Lao Tzu (Old Man, or Old Master) was the keeper of the archives at the imperial court of the ancient capital in what is now the Chinese province of Honan. As a follower of a certain "Way" and as a teacher of the same, he became renowned in the eyes of citizens and the emperor alike as one who could help others be happy, fulfilled, at peace, and right with world. Hearing of his tremendous effect on others, even the great Confucius sought audience with this sage slightly his elder.

All too aware of the potential hazards inherent in what people do with the written word, often twisting and turning it into a set of cultural controls or dogmatic instructions for outward behavior, as opposed to an invitation to yield to an inner conscience and natural disposition, Lao Tzu refused to write down his observations and beliefs.

Eventually, notwithstanding his ardent efforts to teach and show the Way, he became disillusioned with men's and rulers' refusal to follow the path of virtue. So, at the age of eighty, on the back of a water buffalo, he trekked away into the desert to forever leave China and civilization. Upon approaching the western boundary of China, toward what would become Tibet, Lao Tzu was recognized by the keeper of the Western Pass, who had previously met Lao Tzu in a dream.

The keeper implored Lao Tzu to write down his philosophy before leaving humanity for good. Reluctantly acquiescing, Lao Tzu sat at the gate and swiftly composed into word his life's collected wisdom. In five thousand Chinese characters comprising eighty-one sections or poems, *The Book of The Way and Its Virtue or Power* was born. Then, without fanfare, Lao Tzu delivered the text to the keeper of the Pass, climbed atop his water buffalo, and drifted westward into the distant mountains and into history, as the originator of one of the most influential written works of all time.

After being asked by his disciples concerning his visit with Lao Tzu, Confucius said,

> Birds have wings with which to fly. Fish have fins with which to swim. All the wild beasts have feet with which to run. For wings there are arrows. For fins there are nets. For feet there are traps. But no one knows how dragons make their way through the heavens. Today I have met Lao Tzu. Today I have met a dragon.

That, of course, is the legend, and whether the *Tao Te Ching* was written by this one man or by a collection of sages over a three- or four-hundred-year period, no one knows for sure. As for my part, when I read the words, I see the Old Man writing them. When I try to figure out what the words mean, I see the Old Man living them.

The *Tao Te Ching* and
The Way with Children

Through his teachings, and later through the *Tao Te Ching*, Lao Tzu attempted to address many of the ills of a nation torn by war and social unrest. He saw that a world could be ruled in peace if those who ruled would also follow the Way, or the Tao. By following the Tao, a ruler would be able to reign in peace, and the people would be naturally inclined to obey the reasonable requests of those who governed. This manner of ruling is at once mysterious and evident, illusive and ever present, and only the diligent student would be able to achieve such a level of effortless and natural leadership. Lao Tzu understood how to help leaders lead in this proper manner.

The *Tao Te Ching* sets forth these leadership principles sometimes straightforwardly, other times ambiguously, and other times even elusively. The principles were to be understood as much by letting go of preconceived leadership techniques as by acquiring new leadership concepts. The method of instruction was a process of trying to understand the principles with the help of a masterful mentor.

Revered as one of the all-time most powerful cannons of wisdom on the subject of leadership and governing, used by monks, chiefs, generals, and emperors for centuries, the *Tao Te Ching* is itself a masterful mentor.

The Way with Children
As a student of the *Tao Te Ching* for over thirty years and as one who has worked with "troubled" teenagers in behavioral health programs for nearly as long, the principles set forth in the *Tao Te Ching* have helped me understand how to work with at-risk youth in the same manner Lao Tzu described government leaders can and should work with the populous.

While serving in the lives of literally thousands of teenage children, I have consistently seen how these principles apply in the relationships between those who would help and those would be helped, albeit at first reluctantly. I have seen program staff members who unknowingly yet flawlessly adhere to the principles of the *Tao Te Ching* and, seemingly without effort, gain compliance and cooperation. On the other hand, I have seen well-educated staff members exert great effort, and yet they were unable to gain the least degree of genuine cooperation. Clearly there are modern leaders of children who understand, at least in part, the wisdom Lao Tzu understood so long ago.

My goal in writing *The Way with Children* was to create a transduction of the *Tao Te Ching* into a version directly useful to anyone who works with young people in the role of a leader. Any teacher, school administrator, program staff member, coach, mentor, and especially parent can profoundly benefit by gaining an understanding of the principles illuminated by the *Tao Te Ching*, especially one "translated" into a version just for them.

The Way with Children adheres to the form and spirit of the *Tao Te Ching*, yet is specifically written as if Lao Tzu were addressing an audience of parents or those otherwise serving as leaders of young people.

The Writing

It is interesting to note that the *Tao Te Ching* has been translated into various English versions, one of which can be so different from another that one could easily wonder whether the same Chinese manuscript was referenced for both. For this reason, as I am not a student of the Chinese language itself, I used more than seventeen translations into English of the *Tao Te Ching* (and one famous version that is a transduction itself of previous translations) and referenced many others during the process of developing each and every line of the eighty-one sections of *The Way with Children*.

Additionally, although I was not writing a new version of the *Tao Te Ching*, I wanted to remain faithful to what I believe to be the intent of the actual document, especially when it came to the subject I was seeking to undertake. I wanted to represent, as closely as I could, what I believe Lao Tzu would have written if the keeper of the Western Gate had asked him to write specifically for those who serve in a leadership role with young people, especially teenagers from the twenty-first century. To that end, during the majority of the writing process, I also referenced many hundreds of individual Chinese characters and their English equivalents, which were either single or multiple words.

It is my intention and hope beyond hope that what I have written is what Lao Tzu would have written, if given the chance to write to leaders of youth and parents today.

Using This Book

Understanding it

In some cases, you may feel as if you don't yet understand a particular verse. Such occasions will likely be due to the fact that what is written does not match up cleanly to how you already see things. In such instances, I suggest you leave that verse alone for a while, read other parts, then return to the verse to see if you understand it differently. It has become clear to me that Lao Tzu did not consider it his responsibility to describe the principles in such a manner as to have them agree with anyone's current view, or even apparently to agree with his own, but to share principles, the understanding of which is the responsibility of each individual person who is seeking to walk in the Way.

Exchangeable terms

The purpose of this book is to inform anyone performing the role of a leader of young people. In some cases, you will see that the most obvious subject of a particular section is a parent, but even in those instances, the section can just as easily be written for a coach or a schoolteacher. Each section is written for any person in a position of authority over a child or teenager for any duration of time. So the terms *parent, coach, teacher, instructor, line staff, psychiatric technician, therapist, principal, youth group leader,* and *mentor* are all interchangeable for the purposes of this volume.

Fragments and the whole

Fragments and sentences can be very useful to keep in mind. They provide isolated principles to ponder. Although useful by themselves, the isolated principles are better understood within the context of the whole. And the whole is understood better by rereading the fragments.

The process of reading and rereading

This book is not designed to be read only once. The act of reading it all the way through will inform a new understanding for the next time around. Reading it and having the language of it in your day-to-day awareness invites your brain to look for the principles it alludes to but never fully describes. You will become aware of things happening around you that seem to coincide with the Way.

When you return and read again, you will notice the language illustrating what it was you were feeling or noticing throughout the day in your own behavior. Reading it is a process that grows richer with time.

The book points you in the direction of experiencing Tao. In some cases it does this by being enigmatic and apparently contradictory, in such a manner as to destabilize your current understanding just enough for new understandings to begin to materialize. I have no idea what your understandings will be. If this experiencing were described, it wouldn't be Tao. Indeed, your participation with the book will supply much of the meaning it is trying to convey. Come back to it later to see if its principles have been confirmed and further developed in you.

Ponder
The Way with Children is meant to be less of an instruction manual and more of a tool for pondering and for recentering one's disposition in the world with others, especially with those whom we parent, teach, instruct, or in some other way lead. As you read the book, note sections that draw your attention. Are there sections that inspire, confuse, or even irritate you? When you come across such sections, mark them, go back to them, reread and ponder them. Ponder the fact that Lao Tzu was living in such a way as to make certain conclusions about life, and his attempts to describe these conclusions only show glimmers of a fire of truth he stood well in the middle of. Pondering the glimmers he provides gets us closer to the fire.

Find mentors
Go to individuals who work well with children of all ages and types. Ask them to help you understand sections of this book. These people don't need to know anything about Taoism—in

fact, in most instances, they won't. But as they try to help you understand principles set forth by Lao Tzu, you will see their own innate understanding of the principles flow out in their own language. "Tokens of truth are manifest." (section 21) Take these tokens of truth, and meld them with your next readings of lines from *The Way with Children.*

Repetitive themes
Some topics seem to be addressed repeatedly. What is the message here? One can assume Lao Tzu knew that offering the same teaching in slightly different forms and in slightly different contexts was an important method for finally getting the principles across to students of his work.

Realign
This book portrays an ideal picture of a parent or mentor, but claiming that all parents must have always been and should always remain ideal parents as described is not the point of the book. Let the book serve as a reminder and realigner as you go about performing your duties as a mentor, teacher, coach, program staff, or parent. Let it help you get back on track along the Way. It is meant to inform your next step, not to condemn your past steps.

God
Although he uses the term *God* often, it appears as though Lao Tzu had no interest in defining God. The term seems to be interchangeable with the general meaning of nature or Tao itself. So when the term *God* appears, take it as you wish, and define it as you will. It is such a pervasive theme across the *Tao Te Ching*, I felt compelled to leave it in unapologetically. Your personal and intuitive definition of God might be very similar to Lao Tzu's definition of Tao. Exploring the one, in your own way, may help define the other.

The manner of writing

"Okay this section is giving me the most trouble," said Shayne, sitting at a desk in front of numerous open versions of the *Tao Te Ching* and tapping the pencil's eraser on his forehead with evident frustration. "I really need help. How would you have phrased this section in the context of working with children?"

As was his Way with Shayne, he let many moments pass by, and then Lao Tzu, who could often be found standing softly somewhere behind and to the right of Shayne's peripheral vision, quietly responded, "What's the difficulty?"

Most of the time Lao Tzu wouldn't reply at all, but these were arduous lines indeed, and it was obvious Shayne was in extreme need of elucidation.

So Lao Tzu approached the desk and motioned Shayne to the side. He then studied the section intently for what seemed like years—or minutes—not for his own sake, of course. He himself had written the section, so why should he need to study it?

Yet he peered into it, recapturing the meaning, drawing it forward until his visage held the essence of that specific section. Then he turned to face Shayne squarely and stated intently, as with a twinkle, "You and I have known each other for a long time. Why don't you tell me how I would have phrased it."

Looking back into Lao Tzu's eyes, Shayne saw how the meaning met the new lines, and he responded respectfully, "Thank you. I know what to do now." Then swiftly Shayne put the other end of the pencil to its proper use, while Lao Tzu returned to his proper location.

Dedication

To my mentors
    They showed me
        As they knew the Way

To my children
    They remind me
        As they absorb the Way

To my wife
    She finds me
        If ever I lose the Way

Dispense

The Way to parent according to Tao
    Cannot be defined using words,
        For it is beyond words.

Terms may be used to speak of it,
    But they cannot grasp it.

This Way to lead children according to Tao
    Existed long before
        There were children to lead.

It existed before heaven and earth.
It is the unlimited way to bring up any child.
It lies beyond our limited understanding.

Therefore,
    To see beyond your own boundaries as a parent
        In order to reach the heart of your child,
            Dispense with concepts,
                With techniques,
                With your own desires
                    And expectations.

It is as though this Great Way is hidden—
    A mystery to every leader—
Yet aspects of it may be always manifest
    In simple daily events.

The mystery
    And the manifestations
        Arise from the same source.
Words make these two seem different,
    But the words only express appearance.

If we must name these,
    Let us call them wonder.

From wonder into wonder,
    True parenting and leading unfolds.

3

Regard

Parents,
    Finding one innate thing about their children beautiful
      Will find other innate things ugly.

    When finding some things good,
      Will judge other things as deficient.

Yet in every child
    Seen according to the Tao,
The hidden and the apparent create each other.
The difficult and the easy complement each other.
The tall and the short illustrate each other.
The highs and the lows define each other.
The varying tones give their own music to a young voice.

And the way they will regard others
    Follows the way you regard them.

Hence the Master Parent
    Accomplishes without effort,
    Teaches everything without saying anything,
    Takes their children as they come,
    Serves without demanding,
    Lays no claim,
    Takes no credit.

Because true parents forget themselves
    In the lives of their children,
Their children will never lose the highest regard
    For them.

Clear and Simple

When you over-esteem and lavish praise
    On those children whom you perceive
        As having talent or merit,
            Your children will be full of rivalry and contention.

When you overvalue possessions and belongings,
    Your children will feel the compulsion to covet or steal.

When you constantly stimulate your children's wants,
    Your children will be disturbed.

The sound parent leads children by
    Emptying their minds,
    Opening their hearts,
    Filling their stomachs,
    Relaxing their ambitions,
    Toughening their bones.

In this way the children can have clear thoughts
    And simple needs
And in no way will fall victim
    To any cunning meddlers.

Practice action-nonaction.
    Do not force,
        And you will find
            That without the use of compulsory means,
                Good children will come of themselves.

湛兮其若存

Something Is There

Can people really parent according to the Tao
Like a well
Used without needing to be filled?
Yes.

Can children really be led in such a way
That they continue to see their own infinite possibilities
As though they are origins in themselves?
Yes.

Can leaders of children
Smooth the sharp edges,
Untie tangles,
Temper the glare,
Settle the dust,
Unite a family?
Yes.

In the deep,
In the vastness,
Something is there,
Holding the secrets of true leading and parenting—
Hidden but always present,
Full of questions and answers alike.

I do not know when the Way was conceived.

It came before God.

Inexhaustible Capacity

Heaven and earth are impartial,
Treating the comings and goings of one thing
    As they would another.

Wise mentors are the same.
They regard each child
    Not because of their qualities
        But regardless of them.

The space between heaven and earth is like a bellows—
    Empty and inexhaustible.
The more it moves,
    The more it holds,
        The more it gives.

The wise parent is the same—
    Never confusing personal selfishness
        For personal incapacity.

Try to understand this truth by talking about it,
    The less you will comprehend it.

Simply find it at the center.

Without Effort

The source of knowing how to lead a child
Comes from the valley spirit that never dies,
From the Great Mother,
Who gives birth
To heaven and earth.

This knowing is—
Although behind a veil—
Constantly available.

As a leader, it can become of use to you,
As you will,
Without effort.

Not for Self

Heaven and earth are eternal.
   Why?
Because they do not live for themselves.
   Thus they are present for all beings.

Wise parents put themselves after their children,
   Thereby leading them.

They don't insist on being the center of their children's lives,
   Thereby uniting with them.

They are selfless with their children,
   Thereby fulfilled as parents.

Free of Blame

Parents of the highest good
    Are like water,
Benefiting their children
    And not contending.
They will go wherever they need to go
    In order to arrive at their child—
    A journey most leaders disdain,
        Yielding and low,
            Near the Tao.

In dwelling with your children,
    Build your own solid foundation.
In your thoughts concerning them,
    Meditate deeply.
In your relationship with them,
    Be generous and kind.
In speaking with them,
    Be honest.
In overseeing them,
    Be organized and clear.
In your profession,
    Let them see you working to increase your skill.
In your actions toward them,
    Do things at the right time.

Free of coercion from you,
Free of feeling justified by observing your actions,
    They just might see the Way,
        And you will stand free of blame.

12

Calamity

In disciplining or rewarding,
    A leaders of youth can
Keep filling the bowl to the brim,
    Yet it is better to stop at the right time than to spill.
Oversharpen a sword,
    And now the edge cannot be preserved.
Keep filling their homes with jade and gold,
    Past their abilities to protect it.

Let your children lay their hearts
    On possessions, others' approval, and pride,
        And you bring them calamity.

Following the way of heaven,
    A leader will do the requisite work
        Then peacefully step back.

Only with Your Heart

While interacting with young people today,
    Can you keep your spirit and body in harmony?
    Can you embrace the oneness and never depart from it?
While dealing with young people in the moment,
    Can you focus even your vital breath
    So as to be supple as a newborn?
While seeking to understand young people in your life,
    Can you cleanse your inner vision of blemish
    To see the mystery unobstructed?

Can you love the young people in your charge
    Without manipulating or using cunning?

In all that comes and goes around you
    And your young students,
        Can you remain receptive and open?

Can you with your mind
    Ascertain and discern
        Everything about the lives
            Of the children you lead
                But interfere
                    Only with your heart?

Raise and nourish.
Guide but lay no claim.
Benefit without exacting gratitude.
Lead without controlling.
This is called the Profound Mysterious Virtue.

That Part of Us

Thirty spokes converge.
    The hub is useful only
        Because of the usefulness of the void.

A wall is built up around.
    The clay vessel is useful only
        Because of the usefulness of the void.

Doors and windows are cut.
    The room is useful only
        Because of the usefulness of the voids.

We have to our advantage and benefit
    The knowledge, skills, and talents we possess
        As leaders.

Yet our usefulness to the children
    Comes only when we make use of that part of us,
        Which cannot be measured, isolated, or identified.

Power Within

The five colors can blind a child's eye.
The five tones can deafen young ears.
The five flavors can dull a new palate.

Racing around doing exciting things
    Makes a young person's mind go mad.
Fancy and expensive possessions
    Impede internal progress.

Therefore,
Sagacious parents are examples.
    They cultivate what is within themselves
        And reject external distractions.

They attend to their children's bellies,
    Not their children's eyes,
Helping them to prefer their own power within
    And letting go of the rest.

Entrusted

To favor a child
    Or disfavor a child—
        Both cause trouble.

A child who sees self as self
    Can be hurt.

What does it mean to say that to favor a child or disfavor a child both cause trouble? Because favor becomes sought after for favor's sake, and when disfavored, a child sees favor as fleeting and conditional. Both become found from external sources.

What does it mean to say that a child who sees self as self can be hurt? The reason people suffer hurt is that they are occupied with self. If a person were not occupied with self, how could that person be hurt?

Hence,
    Leaders who regard the student
        As they regard themselves
            Can be entrusted with them.

Charge for the governance of young people
    Belongs to those who care in this way.

While Holding

The power behind being a wise leader of youth
    When looked for in the form of specific techniques
        Will become too elusive to see,
    When listened for in the form of step-by-step instructions
        Will become too rare to hear,
    When grasped for in the form of particular methods
        Will become too small to contain.

The elusive, rarefied, and infinitesimal
    Come together as one unfathomable quality.
This quality of a leader of Tao
    Is not bright on its upper side
        And on its lower side, not dim.

Unnamable, this quality will show itself in practice
    Then will recede back into the undefined realm.

All forms of good parenting, teaching, and leading youth
    Come from this formless origin,
But it is subtle.
    Go to meet it directly; it has no front.
    Seek to follow behind it; it has no back.

The primordial Tao runs like an ever-present thread.
    While holding it,
        You can harness the now
            Between you and a child.
    While holding it,
        The essence of ancient wisdom is yours.

When you let it go,
    Your ability to lead youth
        Becomes inaccessible again.

Understanding this is finding the beginning.

Simply Appears

Masterful leaders of old were subtle and profound—
So much so that they are incomprehensible to us.
We can merely describe their appearance:
    Cautious like one crossing an icy stream,
    Alert like one surrounded by enemies,
    Yielding like melting ice,
    Genuine like uncarved wood,
    Open like a valley,
    Churned like a muddy torrent.

Churned?

Can you,
    Like these ancient masters,
        Still yourself in the midst
            Of the children's churning torrents,
                Awaiting tranquility?

A constant calm stream allows mud to settle by itself,
    Revealing
        The proper responses,
        The right actions.
            As though they simply appeared.

Parents of the Tao don't seek fulfillment.
    This is precisely why they feel complete.
Though their children constantly employ their efforts,
    They understand how to not need renewal.

However Fine

Teach children this:

"Do your best to attain the emptiness of humility.
Do your best to hold on to the stillness of peace.

As the ten thousand things rise and fall,
    As the myriad creatures flourish,
Watch these and contemplate them.
    Witness how each returns to its root.

To return to the root
    Is called finding stillness.
To find stillness
    Is to return to the mandate of heaven.
To return to the mandate of heaven
    Is to know unchanging principles.
To know unchanging principles
    Is to be enlightened.
Ignoring unchanging principles
    Is willful blindness, the working of evil.

Following constant unchanging principles,
  One sees things as they are.
Seeing things as they are,
  One is impartial.
Being impartial,
  One is capable of kingly justice.
This kind of justice
  Is an expression of the Devine.
Divinity and Tao
  Are the same thing.

Tao is eternal.
  Being one with Tao
    Is to be eternal also,
      Even after your body dies."

However fine your teaching and leading,
  To help young people understand anything less than this
    Is ultimately finite
      And futile.

Highest Order

The parent of the highest order
    Is one whom the children barely know exists.
Next is the parent
    Who is loved and praised.
Next is the parent
    Who is feared.
Worst is the parent
    Who is despised.

If you fail to trust your children,
    They will become untrustworthy.

Master Leaders talk little,
    And in their actions rely on the Tao.
Then,
    When their task of guiding is done,
        The children will say,
            "We have achieved this ourselves."

When Forgotten

When parents or leaders forget the way of the Great Tao,
    They create rules for ethics and justice,
        And the need to teach kindness appears.

When parents use cleverness and strategies,
    Their children sense hypocrisy.

When parents forego natural harmony,
    They become pious
        And expect their children
            To become dutiful and obedient
In the same way that when a nation is reigned in darkness,
    The people are forced to be patriotic.

Internal Matters

Give up your religiosity and your own wisdom.
    Your children will benefit a hundredfold.

Upon discarding your assumed morality and brand of justice,
    Your children will have opportunity to see naturally
        The right thing.

Abandon profiteering and shrewdness,
    And the less likely your children will find reason to steal.

These are, however, external matters
    Insufficient in themselves.
        Most important is what happens inside you.

See the purity in your children.
Embrace responding to what is simple about them:
    Their dreams, fears, needs, and desires.

Diminish your own self-interest.
Subordinate your desires to those of your family.

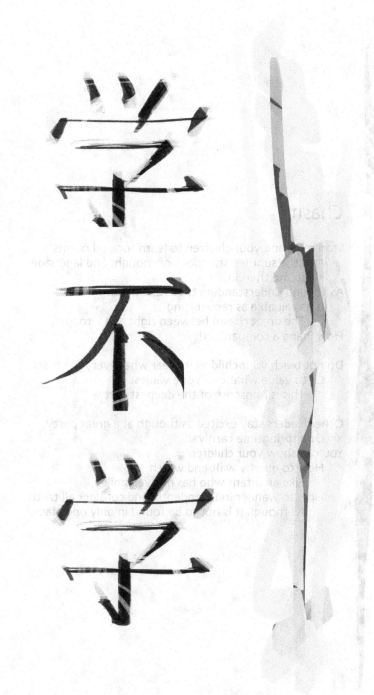

Chasm

Stop requiring your children to learn societal norms
And the subtle distinctions of thought and language
found therein,
As though understanding these distinctions
Is as valuable as recognizing
The great chasm between right and wrong.
How inane a comparison!

Do not teach your children to fear what everyone fears
Or to value what everyone values.
This is nonsense of the deepest sort.

Other leaders stay excited as though at a great party
Or a springtime carnival.
You can show your children
How to quietly wait and watch
Like an infant who has not yet smiled,
How to wander independently and consider all truth
As though it is not to be found in only one place.

Other leaders have more than they need.
You can show your children
    The value of not needing,
    The value of not supposing.

Other leaders shine brightly.
You can show your children
    The apparent dimness of humility.

Other leaders are sharp minded.
You can show your children
    How to be ignorant of such things
    And instead to drift on the vastness of the ocean,
        Everywhere the wind can go.

Other leaders fix on a goal and stick to it.
You can show your children
    How to be stubbornly free from stuckness.

Help them have the unconventional experience
    Of being nourished directly from nature herself.

Forms of It

As a leader of youth,
  The greatest virtue I can have
    Is to follow the Way and the Way alone.

Learning to lead according to the Way
  Is an elusive and intangible achievement.
    But I have seen forms of it.

Intangible and illusive as it is,
  I have seen substantive evidence of this capacity:
    Flashing images and masterful moments
      With children
        By leaders while in the Way.

Evidences for their capabilities
  Seem to come out of the shadows,
    Only to return back into the dimness.

When an act of leading in the Way occurs,
  Although immeasurable,
    It is genuine and real.
      Tokens of truth are manifest.

These tokens have existed from the beginning,
  And their names haven't changed.

How do I know this?

Because this phenomenon has always spoken for itself!

Broken

If you want to be a leader of youth
    And a truly competent parent:

Let yourself be whole
    By allowing yourself to be broken.
Let yourself retain straightness
    By allowing yourself to bend.
Let yourself be filled up
    By allowing yourself emptiness.
Let yourself become renewed
    By allowing yourself to wear out.

Teach your children to have little
    So they might receive much.
Having a lot just confuses them.

Masterful leaders embrace the Tao
    And truly become patterns for the young:
        Not displaying,
            The children see their light;
        Not justifying,
            The children trust their words;
        Not self-asserting,
            The children recognize their merit;
        Not prideful in being,
            The children allow their influence to endure;
        Not contending,
            The children surrender to their invitations.

The Ancients proclaimed:
"Let yourself be whole
    By allowing yourself to be broken."

This is not just some idle saying!

For if you really do become whole,
    Competencies with children
        Will come to you of themselves.

Trust Cultivated

Like nature,
   A parent of Tao
      Is sparring with words.
Gale force winds do not last long.
A sudden heavy rain does not outlive the day.
What causes these two conditions?
   Heaven and earth.
If heaven and earth refrain from endless goings-on,
   Should not parents also?

If parents cultivate the Tao,
   They will become one with it.
If they cultivate virtue,
   They will become one with it.
If they cultivate loss,
   They will become one with it.

When you are one with Tao,
   Your child will feel welcomed to you.
When you are one with virtue,
   Your children will feel your stability for them.
When you are one with loss,
   Your children will not feel forced to return.

These things exist at the same time:
   Fail to be trustworthy
   Or fail to trust your children
      And your children will become untrustworthy
      And will fail to trust you.

Excess Baggage

Standing on tiptoes,
    Overreaching parents remain unsteady
        For their family.
Striding for the faster pace,
    A straining mother will not get far
        With her child.
Kindling to show his own brilliance,
    A flickering teacher does not shine well
        In his students' eyes.
Justifying his own conduct,
    A self-acquitting father forfeits the respect
        Of his daughters and sons.

Boasting of her many achievements,
    A self-admiring instructor has no merit
        With her pupils.
Clinging to the success of his work,
    The work of a prideful leader will not endure
        In the lives of the younglings he would lead.

The simple heart of a child and creation itself
    Detest these behaviors.
The natural soul of a young person
    Sees them as excess baggage—superfluous actions.

When teachers, leaders, or parents
    Aspire to the Way,
        They cease giving place to such inner folly.

Least Experienced

There is something mysterious
    That can inform the least experienced leader of youth
        To govern in the most complete and perfect manner.

The source that informs
    This right Way of governing children,
        Although without apparent structure
            Or steps to follow,
                Is complete and perfect.

This mystery existed before heaven and earth were born.
    It silently stands alone,
        Unfailing, unchanging.

It flows through all things.
    This is why it can inform
        Teachers, leaders, and parents alike.

It may be regarded
    As the Mother of all things.

I don't know its name,
    So I name it Tao.

If I had to describe it,
    I would call it Great.

Great means flowing onward;
Flowing onward entails going far away;
Going far away implies a returning.

Therefore Tao is great.
Heaven is great.
Earth is great.
A leader of youth
    Aligning with Tao
        Is great.

These are the four greats
    In the universal realm,
        And the person of Tao is one of them.

Tao is so of itself,
Heaven follows the pattern of Tao;
Earth follows the pattern of heaven;
A person who follows the pattern of earth
    Is a leader of Tao.

A child's heart
    Is naturally drawn
        To that which is great.

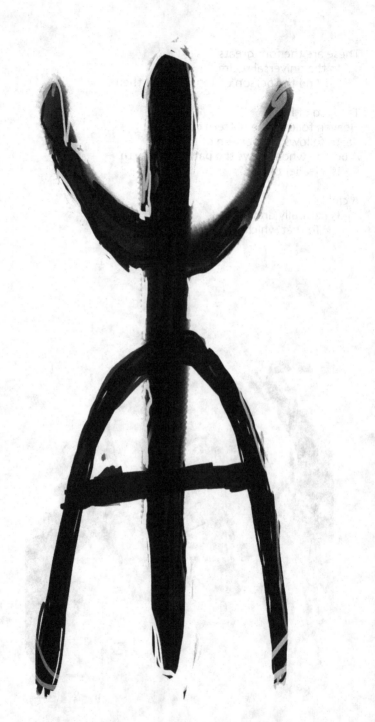

Restless

Heavy is the root of light.
Contentment is the master of restlessness.

Therefore, Master Parents, while traveling,
    Will yet stay focused on their starting place.
Though there may be splendid sights to see,
    They prefer their own home.

Why should those who have the duty of a parent,
    Which is more important than being the lord
        Of ten thousand chariots,
            Behave as though their duty were light.
Parents who thusly act lightly
    Separate themselves from their own root.

The parent who is restless has lost self-mastery.

Yielding

A good walker leaves no tracks.
A good speaker leaves no occasion for criticism.
A good reckoner uses no counting rods.
A good closer shuts a door.
    And even without bolt or lock,
        Closed it remains.
A good tier ties a knot.
    And even without rope
        Bound it remains.
Therefore the sage leader of youth
    Is always good at saving children:
        No one is abandoned;
    Is always good at saving things:
        No thing is abandoned.
This is called
    Yielding to the light
        Of one's inner intelligence.

While residing in the Way,
    A person is good.
While not residing in the Way,
    A person is bad.

Surely the good person is the bad person's teacher;
And the bad person is the good person's charge.

Those who seek to mentor children
    Must be good
        Or must quickly seek
            To be a good person's charge,
Because without goodness,
    Instead of mentoring children,
        Bad people will cause confusion
            No matter how much they know.

Sooner or later, children respect goodness.
And good teachers always cherish children,
    Even if the children
        Do not yet follow the Way.

This is an essential principle of Tao
    And a mystery to those "leaders of children"
        Who don't want to understand it.

When So Being

Know the masculine nature
　And retain the feminine way,
　　And you will be like a ravine
　　　Drawing down virtue.
Leaders of youth can be this way,
　And when so being,
　　Their childlikeness draws children
　　　To the virtue that is present.

Know the brightness all around
　And retain the dull
　　Like one who has proper perspectives,
　　　Seeing contrasts.
A leader of youth can be this way
　And when so being
　　Upholds a clear standard,
　　　Showing the unerring and limitless path.

Know the honor
　And retain the humility.
　　Like a low valley,
　　　Receiving all things,
A leader of youth can be this way,
　And when so being
　　Holds all-sufficient power of influence.

In this way,
　The Tao would have you
　　As an uncarved block.

Only a block not yet carved
    Can be made into useful implements.

Shaping without chopping,
    The Sage knows how to do things
        With wood
            And with children.

Sacred Vessels

Do you want to take hold of children
    And have them do what you want?
I do not see how you can succeed.

Children are sacred vessels,
    Not made to be tampered with or manipulated.

To tamper with them
    Is to spoil or ruin them.
To grasp them
    Is to lose them.

As a leader with Tao,
There is a time for being ahead of children,
    A time for following behind,
A time for working hard with them,
    A time for being at rest,
A time for being the stronger one,
    A time for being the weaker,
A time to allow for up,
    A time to allow for down.

The Master Parent remains sensitive,
    Seeing children as they are
    Without trying to control them,
    Letting them go their own way,
    Avoiding extremes, excesses, extravagances.

This is residing at the center of the circle.

Battles

The leader who knows how to guide
    Children in the path of Tao
        Doesn't try to influence them with forceful strategies.

Force invites counterforce.

Forceful techniques turn on their wielders,
    Because battles between people
        Are inevitably followed
            By famines between people.

As a parent or leader,
    Simply do what needs to be done,
        Then stop.

Attain your purposes
    But not by pressing the advantage you have
        Because of the position you hold as authority.

Don't measure your ability or success
    By the number of battles you win.
Don't feel proud of how much control you have obtained.
    Rather, regret that you had not been able
        To prevent the war.

Accomplish, yes, but not by overpowering.
To over-press your own agenda
    Is to invite decay of the group, team, class, or family.
This is against the Tao.
    Whatever is against the Tao
        Will soon cease to be.

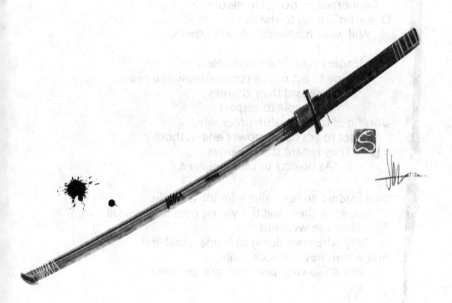

Weapons

Those in authority over "difficult" children
    Can use bewildering techniques for control,
        From rewarding manipulation to punishing coercion.
Such techniques,
    Although brilliantly employed,
        Are weapons of war.

Weapons are instruments of ill omen
    Abhorred by beings in nature.
One who aspires to the Way
    Will want nothing to do with them.

True leaders value the honorable side,
    Seeking to act out of centeredness and peace.
        They regard their charges
            As people to respect.
Unrefined leaders value *other* side.
    Eager to act out of power and authority,
        They regard their charges
            As objects to be conquered.

True leaders do not value winning a battle
    Between them and the young people they lead.
Thus they use weapons
    Only when not doing so is unavoidable.
And when they use such tools,
    They do so with prudence and restraint.

Any leader of young people
   Who delights in having gained a victory
      Over a child in his or her care
         Will not find real success
            With any child in this world.

Deal with affairs of battle between you and children
   As you would a funeral rite.
Mourn the harm
   That may have been inflicted
      By your weapons,
         And seek soon to repair it.

Uncarved Block

The sound leader's way of doing things
    Is nameless and undefined
        Yet constantly limitless.
Like an uncarved block,
    Anything can be carved from it.

Although in its simplicity
    It seems trivial,
        It is inferior
            To not one thing in existence.

If all people in authority over children
    Also possessed this simplicity,
        Centered in the Tao,
            The children would submit
                Of their own accord,

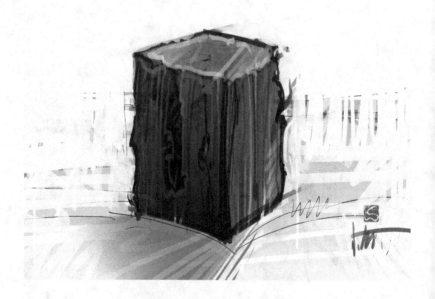

Because what children need
    Would be there,
        Ready to be made,
            As if heaven and earth were conspiring
                On their own
                    To send down sweet dew.

If peace resides in the heart of the leader,
    Children, without being commanded,
        Will treat each other as equals.
            Harmony will naturally ensue.

When complicated leaders appear,
    Seeking to pick apart and define,
        The block becomes carved into pieces.
            A proliferation of names emerges.

When things become
    Institutionalized,
    Perfunctory,
    Regulated,
        Every tiny thing must have a name.

Leaders of Tao know when to stop.

Knowing when to stop
    And to return to the nameless,
        They have preserved themselves
            And the children
                From peril.

A leader of Tao in this world
    Is as a tiny stream to a valley,
        A great river to the ocean.
            Flow goes to the place of no resistance,
                Only reception.

Long Enough

Those who know children
　　Are intelligent.
Those who know themselves
　　Are enlightened.

Those who conquer and control children
　　Exercise power.
Those who conquer and control themselves
　　Are strong.

Those who employ contentment with children
　　Will enjoy wealthy relationships with them.
Those who force their way over children
　　Will find their own willfulness combating willfulness.
Those who, as examples, do not lose their own rooted place
　　Will endure long in the children's hearts.

To truly have lived with the children
　　Until you are no longer with them
　　　Is to have been with them long enough.

Small

People living according to the Way
    Have influence with children universally.

They know what to do with children
    Of all kinds and types,
        From the left to the right.

Resolutions with children depend
    On holding to the Way
        And denying none of them.

Achievements with children depend
    On relying on the Way
        And claiming no merit for them.

Taking care of children depends
    On following the Way
        And holding no authority over them.

Constantly denying none,
    Claiming no merit,
        And holding no authority,
           A person of Tao
               May be called small.

Yet all children are drawn to them,
    And outcomes between them and children
        Flow freely.
           Therefore they may be called great.

Sagacious leaders of youth attain greatness
    By not aggrandizing themselves,
        By not seeing themselves as above the student.
        Therefore, after all,
           They are truly great.

Put to Use

Hold fast to the Great Image,
    And the children will respond to you.

They will trust
    That they will receive no harm.
They will trust
    That they will gain balance.
They will trust
    That they will feel peace.

Music and good food
    Will tempt a passing guest to pause.

But when the Way is practiced
    By teachers, leaders, parents, or mentors,
        When speaking
            They don't sound erudite;
        When observed
            They don't appear sophisticated;
        When listened to
            They don't seem remarkable,

Yet put to use,
    Their efforts are inexhaustible,
        And children cannot seem
            To get enough of them.

Feelings

The teacher who feels punctured
    Must once have been overblown.
The leader who feels vulnerable
    Must once have been armed.
The instructor who feels disrespected
    Must once have been excessively proud.
The parent who feels cheated
    Must once have felt meriting.

Herein is the light of wisdom.
    What you thought
        Was the child's proclivity to offend
    Was in fact
        Your active disposition to be offended.

If you would shrink their anger,
    Expand their vision.
If you would weaken their sting,
    Strengthen their heart.
If you would have them let go,
    Show them what to pick up.
If you would take their resistance,
    Give them something toward which to respond.

Herein is the light of subtle insight:
    The soft and weak overcome
        The hard and strong.

Instruments of sharpness are accessed
    By a leader of Tao
        As often as a fish chooses
            To be out of water.

Way of Being

The Tao doesn't do anything
    By manner of acting.
The Tao does everything needing done
    Through way of being.

If parents, teachers, coaches, and leaders
    Continually abided by the Tao,
        The children will be transformed.

Having been transformed,
    If they falter and begin to act up,
        I would steady them
            With the unnamable natural simplicity.

By steadying them
    With this quality of uncarved wood,
        Children will not feel the leader's desires
            Put upon them.

This stillness of desire
    Invites stillness of desire.

Peace naturally occurs,
    And children correct themselves.

Losing

Truly good parents
    Don't hold a view of themselves as good.
        Therefore they are good.

Parents who hold a view of themselves as good
    Cannot even see their children
        And are therefore good toward them
            Only in false ways.

A truly good parent does not achieve
    Everything that needs to be done
        Through mere action.

False parents are continuously busy with their children
    While accomplishing nothing significant with them.

Kind-hearted parents act
    Without motive,
    Without expectation.
        Few things are left undone with their children.

Just parents act
    With a motive,
    Expecting a fair return.
        Many things are left undone with their children.

Punctilious parents act
    Focused on appropriateness,
        And if they receive no response,
            They roll up their sleeves
                And enforce compliance.

You see,
    Losing the Way with children,
        Leaders will then rely on goodness with children.
    Losing goodness,
        Leaders will rely on kindness.
    Losing kindness,
        Leaders will rely on justice.
    Losing all these,
        Leaders of youth will ultimately rely
            On ethics and rules.

Ethical behavior is the thinnest husk of fealty and honesty.
    The beginning of confusion and chaos
        In one's endeavors to help children.

Extraordinary abilities
    Are only a blossom of the Way.

Masterful Leaders of children
    Dwell on substance,
        Not surface.
They would rather the fruit
    Than the flower.

In order to have grasped the one,
    They have learned to let go of the other.

By the Joining

A leader of youth can be
    Like those that in the most ancient of times
        Naturally joined the Oneness of the Way.

Heaven joined and became limpid.
Earth joined and became stable.
Spirits joined and became potent.
The valley joined and became full.
The myriad creatures joined and became alive.
Those in authority joined
    And became examples for the world.

It is because of the joining that things are what they are.

Without the virtue of the Oneness,
What is limpid becomes obscure;
What is stable becomes fractured;
What is potent becomes exhausted;
What is full becomes empty;
What is alive becomes dead;
Who was honorable becomes fallen.

Hence it is known:
Humility is the root
    From which greatness grows.
That which is high
    Is built upon a foundation that is low.

Prudent leaders call themselves
Powerless, inconsequential, unworthy.
Is this not remaining near the foundation?

Talent is fleeting.
Skill is transitory.
Abilities are provisional.

A chariot is not the sum of its parts
But a product of its wholeness.
The whole is completed
By the joining.

As precious as they are,
The tinkling of jade pendants
Does not compare
To the sound stones make
Deep inside the cliff.

Returning

As a leader of Tao,

Let your movements with children
 Be acts of your own returning to your true self.

Let your usefulness to them
 Be in your quiet yielding to the Way.

Perhaps you will help them see
 The blinding invisible flickering
  Of the not-born source
   Of all born things.

Superior Student

Among those who are parents, leaders, and teachers of youth,
    Some are superior students themselves.
        On hearing of the Way,
            They earnestly put it into practice.

Others are mediocre
    On hearing of the Way.
        They sometimes pitch it up.
        They sometimes put it down
            And consider it short-lived.

Still others are inferior.
    On hearing of the Way,
        They laugh.
            And if perchance
                They hear of it again,
                    They laugh out loud.
If they did not laugh,
    It would not be the Way.

And so the old proverbs thus speak:
    A bright teacher sometimes seems dull.
        And to make no sense,
    A wise leader impels those forward
        Who sometimes think
            They are being led behind.
    When a caring leader holds boundaries,
        Although seen as roughest,
            The easiest way has been provided.

The truly powerful leader lies low like a valley,
    Being the place most easily arrived at
        By those young ones needing to be found.

The teacher who is pure and without guile
    Is often treated ignominiously
        By peers who see only the grim.

The most genuine mentor
    May seem to those
        Who cannot see the Way
           Unreal and fake.

The greatest square has no corners;
    True leaders have no limits.
The greatest vessel is completed late;
    True leader's talents are developed unrushed.
The greatest music is played faintly;
    True leaders speak penetratingly
        Those words of the type
           Only quieted ears can hear.
The greatest image has no shape.
    True leaders build simple beauty,
        Unsophisticated form.

This limitless, unrushed, penetrating, beautiful greatness
    Is what children need to experience.

End

Children are a product
   Of that which birthed all things.

From the Tao is born the one, the two, and the three,
   Then all the myriad beings.

Children feel the warmth of the sun on their backs.
   Children feel the coolness of shade wrapped in their arms.

Their breath helps blend the warm and the cool.
   This blending is a vital part
      Of all of life's harmony and balance.
         This is the vital importance of children.

Young people do not want
   To be alone, powerless, or desolate,
      Yet leaders use words like these
         To express themselves as humble.

Some things diminished find increase.
   Some things increased find diminishment.

What others have taught, I shall also teach.

The influence of
    A leader of youth
        Who carries a violent heart
            Will come to a violent end.

The authority of
    A parent
        Who seeks to lead by force
            Will not come to a good end.

This is the essence of that which has mentored me
    And the essence of my teaching.

Simple Concept

Water offers no resistance,
    Yet a stone can't break it down.
    The reverse *is not* true:
        Water can indeed break down stone.

The softest things overcome the hardest in this world.

Young people who hold up barricades
    Still breathe the very air
        That can easily flow from the other side
            Of the barrier they see as impassable.

A thing without substance
    Requires no space through which to penetrate.

From these two notions, I know the lessons of nonaction,
    Accomplishing without direct action,
    Teaching without words.

Very few leaders of youth
    Understand this simple concept.

The More

Which means more to the child:
    Their reputation or their person?
    What they own or who they are?
Which would cost them more if it were lost?

The more children look
    To the affections of others
        In order to feel fulfilled,
            The deeper will be their suffering.

The more children look
    To the amassing of possessions
        In order to feel happy,
            The deeper will be their loss.

The sound parent
    Does not give the child more
        Than what is enough,
            And therefore the parent prevents disgrace.
The sound parent
    Holds proper boundaries
        By knowing when to stop,
            And therefore the parent prevents peril.

This type of leader
    Would rather demonstrate
        Gratitude and self-restraint.

Thus the leader will long endure.

The Greatest

Perfect mentors seem defective,
 But their usefulness is all-encompassing.

Full mentors seem empty,
 But their efforts are inexhaustible.

The greatest straightness appears crooked.
The greatest skill seems clumsy.
The greatest eloquence sounds like stammering.

Movement is engaging to the cold student.
Stillness is inviting to the hotheaded student.

The mentor,
 Being internally clear,
  Being internally tranquil,
   Helps the student see universal norms
    And how to self-rectify accordingly.

Contentment

When the Way prevails in the world,
Teachers, coaches, parents, and mentors
    Go about performing
        Their appointed duties with children.

When the Way does not prevail,
    Those in authority over children
        Appoint themselves new duties.
These self-appointments
    Coming from a focus on self
        Always come in some form of an act of war.

As a leader of children,
    There is no greater calamity
        Than not knowing self-contentment.
    There is no greater misfortune
        Than the desire for
            Respect,
            Obedience,
            Control,
            Order,
            Self-aggrandizement.

Desiring leader's needs are met
    Through their students' behavior.
        Therefore they demand certain behavior.

Content leaders' needs are met
    By being content.
        Therefore they know contentment.

不

为

而

成

To See

If you are to be the most effective leader of youth,
    Teach this:

"To see what needs to be seen,
    There is no need to open a door
        Other than the one to your own heart,
    No need to peer through a window
        Other than the one to your own soul.

To see what needs to be seen,
    The farther you go away from yourself,
        The farther you'll be from arriving.

To see what needs to be seen
    Requires actions not born of doing
        But born of being."

To teach this you must be one who yourself exemplifies
    Knowing without going anywhere,
    Seeing without looking everywhere,
    Accomplishing by not solely doing.

Alternatives

Pursue knowledge of "what to do" with your children;
   Every day something is added to your list.
Pursue the Tao;
   Every day something is dropped.

The list grows shorter and shorter
   Until you are no longer concerned with your doings
   But instead with your being.

Having arrived at this action nonaction,
   The wellspring of all alternatives
      Becomes available to you.
         Nothing is left undone.

You will sway your children
   By allowing them their own course.

If you still have desires to control them,
   They are out of your reach.

True

Parents who are living in the Tao
    Have no set mind of their own
        But adopt the concerns and interests of their children
            As theirs also.

They are good to their children
    When their children are being good.
They are also good to their children
    When their children are being bad.
This is true goodness.

They trust their children
    When their children are being trustworthy.
They also trust their children
    When their children are being untrustworthy.
This is true trust.

A Master Mother feels the heartbeats of her children
    Above her own.
A Master Father feels the heartbeats of his children
    Above his own.
Then,
    Although their children don't understand why,
        They drop their own agendas
            And look to their parents for guidance.

Dead

From coming into this world and leaving it,
>Three in ten parents are fixated on their own life;
>Three in ten parents are fixated on their own death;
>And three in ten live a life pointed to death.
>>Why is this?
>>>Because they are greedily fixated
>>>On what life can bring them.

I have heard it said
>That a true leader of youth
>>Helps young people
>>>To live truly,
>>>To walk peacefully at heart,
>>>To take no offence
>>>>Even at the tigers and buffalos of this world,
>>>To seek no justification for their own behavior
>>>>Through using those they might battle.

Young people so prepared
>Have no place in them
>>For a tiger's claw to tear,
>>For a buffalo's horn to gore.
>>There is no place for a weapon to pierce,

Because that part of them that needed to die
>Is already dead.

And there is no more space left in them
>In need of dying.

Fit

Existence gives birth to children.
Fit elders nurture them.
The earth shapes them.
Circumstances complete them.

Children venerate the Tao
    When they themselves are fit.
While fit, they are kind and kin
    To the myriad creatures
        Who continually give homage
           To the power that bore them.

Children respect their leaders who follow the Way.
Such leaders do not command or expect it,
    But while fit,
        Children are naturally and spontaneously
           Inclined to give it.

A leader who follows the Way with children
	Nourishes them,
	Nurtures them,
	Shelters them,
	Develops them,
	Matures them,
	Completes them,
	Buries them,
	Then allows them their holy return.

Children can always be reminded
	By those who are fit
		What it means to be fit,
			Having sometimes forgotten.

Welcoming into being
	And claiming no possession;
Benefiting
	Without expecting gratitude;
Mentoring
	Without exercising authority—

These are the profound virtues of the Way
	And of those leaders who to it adhere.

Mother

Existence has a beginning.
This beginning can be called the Mother of all things.

Help the children with whom you work
    Know this Mother of all things,
        The source of
            Wisdom,
            Substance,
            Nonaction.

Understanding the Mother,
    They will have the capacity to know the Mother's Son,
        The objects of
            Proper knowledge,
            Proper functions,
            Proper actions.

But while they gain the capacities,
    Continually take them back to the source.
Doing this,
    You will in no way self-imperil.

Help them block the passages
    To their desiring of outside things
        That stimulate the senses.
Doing this,
    You will in no way self-enslave.

Teach them to keep the passages open.
    Teach them to run around this way and that.
Doing this,
    You will assuredly lose your salvation.

A clear eye perceives the subtle and small.
Tender strength is the truest strength of all.

Demonstrate to them how to use their own light
    And to thereby return to the source of all light.
Doing this,
    You will not self-ruin.

This is practicing constancy with children.
This is practicing the Tao with children.

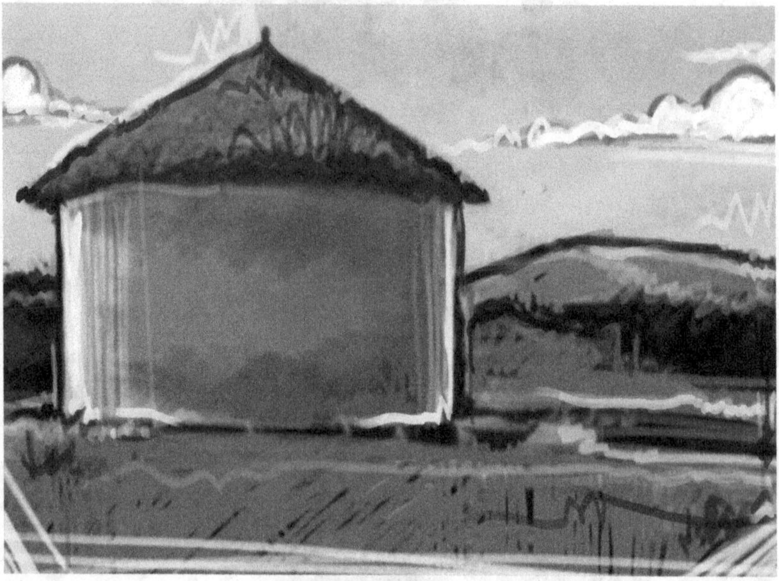

Sidetracked

The parent with the tiniest grain of wisdom
    Will choose to walk in the great path of Tao
        And fear only to stray from it.

This great path is very straight and easy,
    Yet many mothers and fathers prefer getting sidetracked.
Their attention is on making their houses beautiful
    And filling them with treasures,
And on keeping their courtyards and gardens
    Well kept and clean,
While the fields of their children's souls are full of weeds,
    And their children's hearts are like empty granaries.

They want to wear gorgeous clothes
    And drive fancy cars.
They want to eat extravagant food.

When parents spend their time seeking to possess
    More things than they can use
        And then set their hearts on those things,
They are to their children
    Robbers and thieves
Stealing time and experiences from them.

As for Tao,
    They don't know the least thing about it.

Self-Evident

What you firmly planted in a child's heart
    By virtue of Tao
        Cannot be uprooted.
What you helped a child fully embrace
    By virtue of Tao
        Will not slip away.

The children of the children you have taught
    May not come to know your name
        But will reverently sacrifice
            At the altar of your offerings.

The child whose heart you have inspired
    May not remember your name
        But will feel virtue founded.

The family of the child you have mentored
    May not come to know your name
        But will notice virtue established.

The community of the child you have stirred
    May not come to know your name
        But will see that virtue has lasted.

The realm of the child you have led
    May not come to know your name
        But will observe that virtue has become abundant.

The world that encounters
    The children you have influenced
        May not come to know your name
            But will perceive a vast influence indeed.

Hence the children identify their virtue as their own
And the family's virtue as its own
And the community's virtue as its own
And the realm's virtue as its own
And the world's virtue as its own.
    This is enough.
        You recognize it has nothing to do with you.

How can I know about a leader of youth such as you?
You are self-evident.

Troubled Teens

A causer of offense tends also to be
    A taker of it.
A newborn baby causes no offense
    And takes none either.
Taking no offense,
    Things that would normally cause harm
        Don't.

Teens while troubled act like
    Wasps, scorpions, serpents,
    Beasts, and dangerous birds.
If for them you are like a newborn,
    Wasps, scorpions, and serpents don't sting you.
    Fierce beasts don't seize you.
    Birds of prey don't tear you.

Teens while troubled
    Are slippery and hard to hold on to.
If for them you are like a newborn,
    Though ostensibly weak,
    Though ostensibly soft,
        Your grip is unfailingly firm.

Teens while troubled
    Are unbalanced.
If for them you are like a newborn,
    You don't yet differentiate
    The yang from the yin.
        Yet you are naturally whole
            And your essence perfectly mixed.

Teens while troubled
    Are internally disharmonious.
If for them you are like a newborn,
    You can howl all day long
    Without getting hoarse.
        This is perfect harmony.

To know harmony is to be constant;
To be constant is to be enlightened.

Don't try to gain unnatural benefits.
    Instead,
        Benefit and take what comes.

Don't set your heart on being powerful.
    Instead,
        Power your heart.

Exercising power
    Cannot be called the Way.
What cannot be called the Way
    Is transient and will die soon enough.

Mysterious Sameness

Among leaders of young people there are two types:
    Those who know
        Far more than they talk about and
    Those who talk about
        Far more than they know.

If you are among those who know,
    It is because you have long learned
        What it means to
            Restrain your mouth,
            Close your doors,
            Blunt your sharpness,
            Untangle your knots,
            Temper your shininess,
            Mix with the dust.

This is called mysterious sameness
    Or the capability to unite with those in your care.

Therefore,
Since you don't need them to be close to you,
    You are not mal-effected when they go away.

Since you don't require them to benefit you,
    You are not harmed when they don't.

Since you don't value them valuing you,
    You are not taken aback when they are despising.

Therefore,
    Young people will find value in you;
    Young people will honor you;
    Young people will revere you.

Observances

If you want to lead a group of young people,
   Govern them with forthright correctness.
      Trickery and craftiness are for battling not governing.
Win them by not intermeddling.

How do I know this?
By these observances:

Force prohibition
   And the less self-virtuous children will be.
Wield manipulative weaponry
   And the less self-secure children will be.
Appease by subsidizing
   And the less self-reliant children will be.
Command by rule and law
   And the less self-controlling children will be.
Influence with cunning
   And the less self-aware children will be.

Hence the sagacious leader of youths wisely states:

"I practice noncontrivance
    And sensing authenticity,
        The children transform themselves.
I practice tranquility
    And sensing peace,
        The children order themselves.
I practice forbearance
    And sensing no weightiness,
        The children prosper themselves.
I practice letting go
    And sensing no insistence,
        The children return to themselves."

Profuse Stupidity

When a leader of youth
    Governs with unobtrusiveness and listlessness,
        The children will be wholesome and happy.

When a leader of youth
    Governs with meddlesome astuteness,
        The children will be anxious and cunning.

It has been said,
    "Bad and good
        Give rise to one another
            And lurk beneath one another.
    The enlightened man knows
        There is no real right and wrong."

No one knows the limit
    Of profound and profuse stupidity,
        Such a "wise" declaration promotes.

In a world where straightforwardness
    Is twisted to seem crooked,
        And goodness is assigned strange derivations,
        Know that the bewilderment
            Has lasted a long time.

Therefore the Master Leader
   Brings about square honesty
      Without cutting;
   Probes to reveal all angles
      Without harming;
   Straightens the crooked parts
      Without imposing;
   Lights up the dark corners
      Without shining.

Kingdoms

In governing young people and serving heaven,
    A leader must have stores saved up.
This saving up of stores
    Means absorbing beforehand
        That which redoubles itself.

Accumulated virtue comes
    By following the Way.

Possessing an abundance of virtue,
    A leader sees endless possibilities.

One who sees endless possibilities
    Has no limits.

One with limitless ability
    Will be seen by young people
        As fit for leading them.

They will then give over their kingdom.

But now, with that newly gained kingdom,
    The leader must remain at one
        With the Mother of all kingdoms.

This is called having deep roots
    And a firm foundation.

With such a clear vision of the Way,
    The leader's influence will endure.

Fish and Demons

True parenting is like cooking a small fish.
    Meddle little,
    Just stay in the Tao,
    And you won't ruin anything.

Lead your children in accordance with Tao
    And demons will lose their power.
Not that demons go away,
    But you have ceased opening doors to them.

When you have ceased opening doors to them,
    You have ceased doing harm to your children,

When you cease doing harm,
    You might finally have allowed goodness
        An open channel between you.

以德报怨

Silently Seeking

Great leaders of youth
   Are like low-lying land.
      They draw children to them
         Like streams flowing downhill.

An adult can always achieve this
   By being humble, watchful, and accepting.
      And these come by refusing to be offended.

Children hope for acceptance and understanding.
   This is their natural disposition,
      Even if the opposite, at times, seems true.

So the adult bows voluntarily
   To the child who is inclined naturally
      To bow back without compulsion.

The teacher now is free to instruct
   The students who have now found the mentor
      For whom they have been silently seeking.

Both have accomplished their goal,
   But it begins with the lowness of the leader.

Words and Gifts

Tao is at the source of the universe
    And is secretly present among the myriad creatures.
        It is treasured by those who are good;
        It is a refuge for those who are bad.

Leaders of youth should be like the Tao.

Well-placed words by a child
    Win your respect and honor.
Good behavior is convincing,
    Like presenting you a gift.
But does that mean a bad-acting child
    Should be discarded?

Therefore,
    When you find yourself put in a place of authority
        Over young people,
            Don't cajole or coerce them to run to you
                To show you these words and gifts.

Instead,
    Allow them stillness.
        Experience the Tao with them.

Why did the Sages of old
    So prize the Way?

Because by venturing to be one with it,
    The seeker will indeed find,
        And mistakes will be forgiven.

This is true for parents and children alike.
    That is why
        Tao is so valuable
            To both.

Astounding Effort

Leaders who know the Way
    Act without making the action happen.

They effect
    Without enforcing.
They understand the students
    Without knowing details about them.
They make children who think themselves small
    See their own greatness.
They make a child's multiplicity of qualities
    Self-apparent.
They requite a student's anger
    With integrity.
They see simple resolutions
    Before children's problems complicate themselves.
They accomplish great things in the life of children
    Through small and simple acts with them.

Solutions to the difficult problems with children
    Are found within simple principles.
Big things are accomplished with children
    By doing small things often.

The wise leader achieves greatness by knowing
    That the children's greatest changes
        Ultimately have nothing to do with the leader.

Again:
Commit lightly to children;
    You will inspire little confidence.
Go into it thinking it should be easy;
    It will soon turn difficult.

The Master Leader prepares
    As though the journey with the child
        Will require astounding effort
            And so reaches the end
                Without difficulty.

A Thousand Miles

The day may come
   When your child becomes restless and uneasy with you.
Before this day,
   Hold your heart as close to his as you can.

The day may come
   When dire portents arise in the life of your child.
Before this day,
   Forestall by planning well.

It is while your children are still fragile
   They need learn to be strong.
It is while your children are still small
   They need learn how not to get lost.

Engage yourself in the prevention of trouble
   Long before it exists in them.
Cultivate peace and order in yourself
   Long before they have a chance to become confused.

The tree that will be your child's life
   Starts as a sprout you plant.
She will someday stand atop
   An earthen tower nine stories high
     That started with a clod in your hand.
Your journey with her of a thousand miles
   Starts now from beneath her little feet.

It's not about action;
   Actions can harm.
It's not about control;
   Grasp is easily lost.

Knowing this, the Parent-Sage
   Does not act without also being true
     And through true being
      Invites with power
       In the place of forcing.

Right at the end
    Of the child's formative years,
        Many parents will recognize
            Their own failure.
So take great care,
    As much at the very end
        As from the beginning,
            And in every moment along the way,
                And you will find success.

As the example, Parent-Sages
    Are not self-focused,
    Do not desire precious things,
    Study by unlearning
        The unteachable.
They help their children recover
    Their own true nature,
        If ever they should lose the course.

This they do by being according to Tao,
    Not solely by taking action.

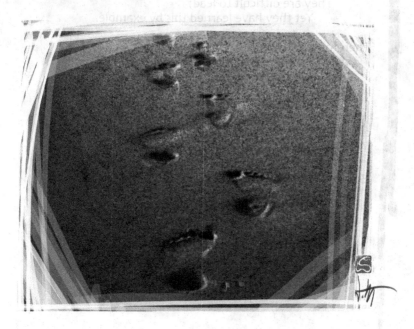

111

Natural Simplicity

In the days of old,
    Parents who practiced Tao
        Didn't try to enlighten their children
But instead
    Wanted to maintain
        Their children's simplicity
           And naturalness.

When children have been taught to be clever,
    To rely on the intellect,
        They are difficult to lead;
           Yet they have learned this by example.

Therefore,
    When parents govern with cleverness,
        They are a curse to their children;
    When they govern with natural simplicity,
        They are a blessing to their children.

To understand these two alternatives
    Is to possess subtle yet penetrating insight.

Employing such insight,
    Parents can show their children
        How to return to their own true nature.

Contend

A true parent
   Is like the sea.
The sea is king of all streams,
   Because it lies below them.

If you wish to guide your children,
   Humble yourself in your speech toward them.
If you wish to lead your children,
   You must learn how to put yourself behind them.

In this way,
   Masterful Parents stand above their children,
     Yet their children feel no weight upon them.
   They go ahead of their children,
     And their children do not feel hindered.

Toward this kind of parent,
   A child feels gratitude
     And a willingness to yield.

No child can contend
   With a parent who will contend
     With no child.

Three Treasures

Almost all practitioners, leaders, and parents
　　Say this Tao way of working with children
　　　　Is great but inconceivable
　　　　　　And inapplicable.
It is exactly because it is great
　　That it seems this way.
If it were easily conceived
　　Or applied,
　　　　How small would it have always been.

There are three treasures
　　To be held and protected
　　　　By those who would help or lead children:
　　　　　　The first is having compassion;
　　　　　　The second is living in simplicity;
　　　　　　The third is daring to not be the boss and foremost.

With compassion,
　　Leaders can confront courageously.
With unencumbered living,
　　Leaders are free to expand their capacity.
With humility,
　　Leaders can be accepted as having such.

To be courageous without being compassionate,
To attempt expansiveness without simplicity,
To be in front without being humble
　　Is to,
　　　　In one way or another,
　　　　　　Court death.

Only with compassion
　　Will we help the children prevail
　　　　In their own inner battles.
Only with compassion
　　Will we help the children build
　　　　Their own inner bulwarks.

Heaven hopes to endow would-be leaders with compassion,
Thereby protecting them from their own destruction
This is for the sake of the children.

Awakening

A good leader
    In authority
        Is not the aggressor.

A good parent
    In disagreeing
        Never gets angry.

The best way of winning over children
    Is not through
        An antagonization
        Or battle.

The best way of employing their efforts
    Is to put yourself below them.

This is called
    The virtue of noncontention.
This is called
    Awakening young ones
        To their own abilities.
This is called,
    As of old,
        Being committed to heaven
            And to the children.

Deft Employment

Masterful parents follow the strategist's saying:
"Do not be the aggressor;
Rather, accept the conflict as it comes."

It is better to retreat a yard
Than to advance an inch.

By the same parents this is called
Moving closer to your children
Without marching your cause over them,
Watching their anger
Without attacking their person,
Exhausting their blows
Without using weapons.

If they present themselves as an enemy,
It is only because they have conflict
In their own heart.
There is no greater misfortune
Than to underestimate the strength
Of this conflict they endure
Or of your own contribution to it.
Underestimate in this way,
And you forsake your three treasures.

When young people oppose you,
Only by yielding to them
With the deft employment of compassion
Will you win.

Understand This

Some people are Master Leaders and Mentors.
Their explanations of how to lead according to Tao
  Are very easy to understand,
    Very easy to put into practice.

Yet you can't *simply* understand their words.
  You can't *simply* put what they say into practice.

For their words come from ancestral rulers.
Their actions stem from ancient origins.

If you cannot understand this,
  You cannot understand them.

Yet observe them, and you shall see
  They are of the few
    Who are completely humble
      While carrying the finest treasure
        In their hearts.

Sick

Some parents and leaders
    Begin to regard their "knowing"
        What is best for children
            As ignorance or not knowing.
This is great insight.

Some regard their own ignorance
    As knowing.
This is mental sickness.

Only when parents and leaders
    Become sick of their sickness
        Will they be able to rid themselves of it.

Master Mentors seek
    To be healed of their own knowledge.
They are sick of sickness
    Between them and the children they lead,
        And thus they discover health.

Without Dwelling

If your children fear your power,
    What you suppose you have
        Is not really power at all.

Respect them in their own lives.
    Turn meddling into trust,
        And perhaps they will not grow weary of you.

Master Fathers and Mothers
    Know who they are
        Without dwelling on themselves.

They love themselves,
    But this is because they love their children
        And everyone else.

They attend to the concerns of children and heaven
    As though these concerns were their own.

Two Kinds

Those who are courageous out of daring are killed;
Those who are courageous out of love survive.

The Parent who seeks order by yelling for it
    Has no peace;
The Parent who seeks order by being at peace
    Finds it.

Of these two kinds of courage and order,
    One is harmful,
    While the other proves beneficial.

Some ways are simply detested by heaven,
    But who knows the reason.
    Even the Sage is awed at this question.

A leader with the Tao
    Knows the way of heaven and children
        To overcome
            Without contention,
        To respond and get responses
            Without speaking,
        To induce a child to arrive
            Without summoning,
        To accomplish without a plan
            Everything that needed to be planned for.

A True Parent's arms are stretched out far,
    As vast as heaven's net.
        Though the meshes are wide,
            The child's most silent petitions
                Don't slip through
                    Unrecognized.

Hacking

If children don't love life,
  They won't fear the effects of punishment
    Or consequences,
      And threatening them with these won't work.

If children have lives worth living,
  The reality of consequence has meaning.
They will do what's right
  To avoid losing the life they cherish.

Punishing a child should be the province
  Of God only
  Or of a parent who is living according to Tao.
For only then would any impositions be lain
  From a parent to a child
    With the wisdom of heaven itself.

For leaders to take "consequencing" into their own hands
  Without residing
    At that very moment
      In the Tao
        Is like hacking at wood
          In the place of a master carpenter.

You would be indeed lucky
  Using his tools,
    Of which you are not familiar,
      Not to cut your own hand.

Enjoy

What makes children look elsewhere
    For attention or belonging?
        Parents eating up all the time they could spend
            Involved in their own concerns.

What makes children rebellious?
    Fussy parents who can't stop controlling
        Or who have private ends to serve.

What makes children fear death or take it to lightly?
    Parents who are bothered by their children,
        Considering some things in life too seriously.

Parents who enjoy their children
    Abide in the depths of wisdom,
        And their children will enjoy their own lives.

Bend

At birth, people are soft and supple;
    At death, rigid and hard.
When a plant is living, it is soft and yielding;
    When dead, stiff hard and brittle

Therefore,
    Parents who are hard and inflexible
        Are friends to their child's death;
    If soft and yielding,
        Friends to their child's life.

An unyielding army will fall to defeat;
An unbending tree will break.

Hard leaders must humble themselves,
    Recognize the ways in which they need to bend,
        Or find themselves otherwise laid low.

Yielding parents will ultimately be exalted
    In the eyes of their children.

Bow

A parent with the Tao or the Way of heaven
    Is like the drawing of a bow:
        The top gets bent downward.
        The bottom gets bent upward.
        The narrow space widens.
        What has too much is diminished.
        What has too little is supplied.
        Perfect balance reigns naturally.

Parents without the Tao are different.
    They are without balance themselves
Because of this.
        Actions within degrees of control or indulgence
            Seem to be their only choices.

Therefore,
    They invite either deficiency or excess
        In the life of their child.

What kind of parents have genuine abundance
    To give to their child?
Only those of Tao,
    Freely drawing
        From among possibilities
            Beyond apparent polarities.

Master Leaders simply stay in the Tao.
    They do not act in order to gain
        What they expect
            From their children.
    They accomplish and lay the credit
        At their children's feet.
    They see themselves
        As their children's equals.
    They wish their merits to be seen
        Only by God.

Water

Not one thing under heaven
    Is greater than a father or mother
        That knows how to be like water,
For nothing is so soft and yielding.
    Yet for attacking hard and inflexible things
        There is nothing like it.

Nothing can compare
    To parents who face difficulties with their children
        In this way.
The yielding father overcomes the strong obstacles
    Between himself and his children.
The soft mother overcomes the hard problems
    Between herself and her children.

Everyone knows this is true;
    But it seems none have the ability to practice it.

Therefore the Sage says:
    Parents who seek to see and accept
        The center, the basic soul of their child,
            Without themselves in the way
                Become masters
                    In sustaining them.

When parents truly bear the evils
    Experienced by their children,
        They become kings and queens under heaven.

The truth is hard to see
    If leaders focus on its opposite.

133

Reconcile

Seek to reconcile resentments you have with your children.
Ill feelings will linger.
What possible good can that bring to you
Or to them?
Rather,
Let resentments go;
Lay no blame;
Take no offense.

The Master Parent holds no tally.

Fulfill the part of the covenant you made
In that you bore your children,
But never lay claim to them.
Be a truly virtuous parent
By concerning yourself
Only with what you owe your children,
Never taking note
That they owe you anything at all.

The Great Way of heaven precludes no one.
It stands like a pillar
Supporting those who wish to lean on it.

Home

Let there be homes governed in great wisdom.

Let a family have modern things,
    Yet not become dependent on them,
        Using them with sound judgment.
Let each member be mindful of death,
    So they stay close to the innocence of youth.
If there be cars and boats,
    Let there be no place more desirable to go.
Let there be no arguments
    Or displays of hostility.
Let each person's responsibilities be few enough in number
    They can be remembered by knotting a string.
Let meals together
    Be enjoyable.
Let all be content with their clothing
    And satisfied with their house.
Let all take pleasure in building
    And living simple family customs.

And though there be other houses so close
   One can hear the barking of their dogs,
   The crowing of their roosters,
Let the children grow up
   Without ever feeling compelled
      To want to spend their time there
         More than at their own home.

信言不美

Example

Useful words are not elaborate;
Elaborate words are not useful.

Good parents don't argue with their children;
Parents who argue with their children aren't good.

A person who knows how to be;
    A good parent
    A good leader
    A good mentor
    A good teacher
        Isn't full of facts about it;

A person who is full of facts about;
    Parenting
    Leading
    Mentoring
    Teaching
        Doesn't know how good one.

Master Paren   oard possessions.
The more th   work for their fellow human beings,
    The fuller their lives become.
The more they give of themselves,
    Setting the example to their children,
        The more their life will abound.

Master Parents, Leaders, Mentors, and Teachers
    Follow the Way of heaven and the Sage.
        They benefit all,
            Harm none.
        They work for all,
            Contend with none.

About the Author

M. Shayne Gallagher has more than a quarter century of experience designing and operating behavioral health and addiction treatment programs for adolescent children. He has been a lifelong student of The Tao Te Ching, applying its precepts to a career of working with those who work with children. He and his wife, Sheri, have six children and live in the four corners area of the southwest.

Printed in the United States
By Bookmasters